The Unwritten Sky

Stories, the Stars forgot to tell

Varnika

BookLeaf
Publishing
India | USA | UK

Made with ❤ on the BookLeaf Publishing Platform

www.bookleafpub.in

www.bookleafpub.com

Dedication

*To my parents, my younger brother, and my best friend
whom I pestered endlessly to read my poetry and
who kindly gave their feedback.*

*To the beautiful readers who have come to explore the
words of this unknown poet.*

And, of course

To Almighty God.

Preface

I am Varnika, and I have always been captivated by nature. *The Unwritten Sky* — my first published book — is a result of my deep and striking interest in topics that remain, for the most part, a mystery. This collection explores various aspects of natural elements, human behaviour, and sometimes the subtle connections between both.

I discovered my passion for writing poetry about four years ago, and I have been writing ever since. While I don't have any formal or in-depth training in literature, this book offers a window into my raw thoughts. As I have not yet turned 18, this collection is, in many ways, a reflection of my thoughts from my minor years — an exploration of my mind during this formative period.

As this is my debut work, I am both excited and nervous to share it with the world.

Through *The Unwritten Sky*, I hope to connect with readers who, like me, find meaning in the small details of life and discover peace in the beauty of the natural world. In sharing these poems, I offer a glimpse into my heart and mind, as well as the stories I have gathered from my own life.

I am deeply grateful to all those who have supported me on this journey, and I thank you, the reader, for taking the time to explore these poems.

Acknowledgements

I would like to extend my heartfelt gratitude to my parents for their endless love, support, and belief in me. Thank you for encouraging me for this project.

Along with my sibling and best friend, I would like to acknowledge my own efforts and success in management of time from a busy academic schedule to write these poetry. Indeed it has been a good time to de-stress, allowing me to jot down whatever has been on my mind lately.

A special thanks to all the readers who have chosen to dive into these poems, giving this unknown poet the opportunity to share these words with the world. Your time is invaluable, and I'm immensely grateful to host a few minutes of your life.

I would also like to acknowledge the countless moments of inspiration that have come from the world around me — from the clear starry nights to the bustling of the day, these moments have found their way into these words.

Lastly, I am forever grateful to Almighty God, whose guidance and inspiration have helped shape the heart and soul of this collection.

1. The Song of Life

I wanted to ask if I could,
The reason behind the existence of me,
Or anyone in the hood.

Even Venus is dazzling bright,
Yet nights on Pluto are dull—
Icy plains and frozen sight,
A heart on it, superficial.

I reckon, the universe is unfair;
Subtle secrets of delight are hidden.
Evident are the notions of despair.

Yesterday and tomorrow are different;
Those colourless times will have
A pinch of shades with sentiment.

Freedom from suffering—desired by all,
Scared of fighting, afraid to fall.

The meaning of life is an eternal mystery,
Locked in the maze of the universe,
Far from the depths of history,
Somewhere near the awe of wonders.

2. Palette

Feelings that are grown as a trait
Carries the proof of a volatile fate.
Cage not your emotions, set them free,
For they may hurt you silently.

Sunrays on the sea, while they shimmer,
Are crystals dancing on the waves.
Joy that builds immense wonder,
A path of serenity that it paves.

A timeless river of love that flows
Carves the path of rugged landscapes.
An eternal endlessness to which it grows,
Honour and faith is all it craves.

Who knows emptiness better than the moon?
The scars, he believes, must be the cause.
If only he knew—the reason echoed too soon.
In awe, they wish for his beauty to pause.

A fire that distinguishes under no sky,
Fierce flames that arise when tempers break.
Poison it is, that corrupts without a try,
A scattered mirror and ruins for an empty stake.

The lotus remembers to breathe in marsh,
A wild petal that stuns in a stone too harsh.
A ray that blooms in a dull sight,
Shattering endless despair through its light.

A silent shadow beside your gaze,
A wilted rose that seeks for praise.
Grief clings like a restless shade,
Shifting its form but never fades.

A fog that critically veils the way,
Covering the insights of capable ends.
The known path gradually fades away,
As the hollow fear of an uncertain trail ascends.

The heart still beats, just as before.
All these colours that you may endure–
Their striking spirit we learn to keep
Briefly shallow, steadily they turn deep.

3. Windsong

A messenger of nature with a wild-spirited grace,
A hint of future, vanishes without a trace.
Minister of the heavens, looks out for all,
Life lessons which are yet to recall.

About air, which tends to be in motion,
Attained selfhood while it goes along its notion.
Called-WIND is vividly bold and free,
A force that achieved its own identity.

Breeze whispers the lullaby of wind's might
Caresses your soul through its gentle flight.
Provoke its heart and you will realise-
Of where its power and ruthlessness lies.

A witness of all moments, a narrator for every story,
Supports a feathered life while it hunts for a quarry.
Carries seeds of life toward a destined site,
Sculpts the earth through its invisible might.

This wild-spirited air, which is free,
Cries and roars in a tight span as it flee
Even a force shan't be captivated as you see-
So why should chains assume our glee?

A musician of wonders, a composer for the wood,
Weaves nature's vision like no one ever could.
Plays with rustling leaves through its gentle grace,
It whispers songs that time cannot erase.

4. In its harmony...

Loud crashes of waves, hear my tales,
My truth is kept concealed–
As intensively I narrate the details,
It commands skill in keeping stories sealed.
The soft sand is just there to console,
A silent solace for my loud soul.
These waves keep washing over my feet,
Tidal caresses, each time we meet.

This vast blue expanse of profound treasure,
Its splendour and grace is beyond measure.
Sun bestows, a sovereign glow on its royal might,
While the moon, soothe it into a tranquil night.
I long for endless reasons to seek its relief,
The breeze that flows, is my origin of peace.
I would lay low and quietly hear,
Of what my seagull friends had to say.
We would all unite together,
Complain about world to this abyss all day.

5. Petals that do not Rebel

Greens infilled with ample greys and blues—
This world, which holds enough monotonous hues,
Perhaps must need some shades of spirit,
Like the petals that embrace every visit.

Valiant blossoms, as steady as they stand
In the age of snow or hot blazing sand.
By nature's hand, deep-rooted in the earth,
They thrive and fade, yet prove their worth.

No voice describes the battles won,
None holds a grudge beneath the sun.
Together they grow while clutching their charm;
Despite the cold, their bond feels warm.

A sprout of the globe—its merit is grace.
Fleeting beauty wilts; the norms they embrace.
Hear their murmur, they speak in a breath,
Tales of renewal and hope after death.

6. With Fire, It Flies

As I lay under that secluded tree,
Sleepless, near the dark endless horizon,
A glow flickered and fluttered around me,
With its kind, the radiance had risen.

I glanced upon, in awe, at their gentle light.
Seemingly, these small sparks could shine so bright.
Petite beings; yet they held the power,
To brighten the earth in its darkest hour.

A momentary life of extended hope.
Fragile in form yet boundless in scope.
A breath; soon meant to fade away,
Sustained this domain, in a selfless array.

They can pierce the gloomy mist of night,
At ease, unafraid in their own skin and light.
No excuse they seek, for glowing in endless sky,
Thus I learned to shed fears for the sake of 'I'.

7. Sakura

I desire for no worldly desire,
If I'm privileged to cherish these cherry,
Blossoms, who are like the ashes of fire,
Reminiscent of something extraordinary.

Could falling fate ever be so ethereal?
Transience, after all, had its own beauty.
Fluttering pink hushes in their vast aerial,
Lead this serene wildness like a destined duty.

Silken petals coloured in the tint of moonlight,
Like snow dancing in wind, on a spring night.
Nature had its ways to preach goodbyes.
Tranquil warmness with no tear in eyes.

For these fleeting jewels, time skips the wait.
Skies will blush in pink again,
To release is sorrow and to return is fate,
For endings bloom where new lights remain.

8. Rain's Forgotten Light

Why call it sorrow, who weeps and cry?
Like someone you lost in the abode of sky.
The sound of drops are heard as quiet tears,
Steps on earth, like they have no fears.

When it breaks itself down,
To selflessly heal the town.
Embrace its touch with a mind gentle and free,
It brings far more than you can see.

Solar hymns draped in the fabric of mist,
A blessing of relief while it solely exist.
An arc of rainbow, a bridge naturally divine,
Paints the sky like a fate where wonders align.

Not everything that falls is meant to grieve,
Crystal tears that this globe would joyfully receive.
They shine like transparent mirrors of truth,
Reflects you swinging in the moods of youth.

Emotions displayed by nature through the rain,
The scent of tender dust, a nostalgic refrain–
Evokes the cycle of life in each gentle stream,
Heaven's own spark with a silver gleam.

9. Veil of Snow

In the pure breath of white stillness,
This world becomes a quiet witness;
Of snowflakes falling on the pale bush of trees,
And the scents of serenity carried by the breeze.

In these lazy hours, with the warmth of time,
We wander through the thoughts we seek.
An ideal moment for self to climb,
To unravel truths, we rarely speak.

In this calmness, our soul might collide,
With the idea of peace, we can not hide.
This beauty asks us to pause and breathe,
To explore the world in its tranquil ease.

10. Lost in Lights

Tall blocks of concrete, where puppets work,
Shadows of their sigh always seem to lurk,
Perhaps storms and stress are unable to escape–
Beyond these towers, stories have lost their shape.

Innumerable cafés, shops and halls,
Ignites city's soul behind these walls.
Amidst the chaos and hustles of town,
Solitude wishes to stand, still and frown.

Constellations of buildings that rise up high,
Where elevators have pace of dreams in sky,
Rhythm of footsteps and honk of cars,
Carries their own tale, tuned into silent scars.

Souls without spark are dimmed lanterns,
Vibrant youth, which moves along euphoric patterns.
Paved paths of such realm often see,
The contrary crossover of gloom and glee.

Skin that skims past those unknown,
Bear their own universes in celestial heart–
They meet within fleeting second they own,
Soon vanishes into crowd's tidal art.

Dawn stretches; while yawn is a usual guest.
Headlights fade, a new hustle begins its test.
Untamed mind again crawls to a new goal.
Astonishingly, it reminds of a reason to console.

11. Silent Echoes

A cloud, too full to rain,
Or a seed, planted in the soil's grain,
Like the words we carry, till they fall,
Unspoken, to save the fate of a broken wall.

Unvoiced words, like ghosts, they remain,
Haunt in regrets and shape the pain.
Air not at ease, time bears the weight,
A fuel to grudge, we can not negate.

This load of sensitive burden,
Is no less than a thousand stones.
Voice could be silenced but;
Time cannot remove the prick of thorns.

In this library of unread articles–
Here, silence speaks louder than sounds.
Imprisoned thoughts, which are never visible,
Where every word, in darkness deeply drowns.

12. Leftover's Cry

Once I beheld you, in my tidal lock,
Our intertwined fate, which none could mock.
A silent witness of my rising mountains and seas,
And doom of empires in ancient memories.

Now that I call you again, you recede–
In this heavy silence, year by year you proceed–
Away in vacuum, I extend my cries,
They seem to get swallowed in your empty skies.

My tides trace your glimpse; Desperate!
But I should keep my oceans moving.
When their guide is lost, by choice or fate,
Shall they weep or still rise, unapproving?

Do you wish to vanish entirely, one day?
Will your cratered heart ever remember me?
Like a sudden departure, you keep slipping away,
A betrayal or did time set you free?

Not caged, with me when you were aligned!
Recall how we painted the heavens,
And real wonder was defined.
Its almost time to spin alone, slow yet bold,
For you keep drifting, too far from my aching hold.

13. The Chimes of Time

Time runs in the lap of darkness,
And light, for which it glows–
Once it is forever and suddenly it flows.
Simply merciless as wrath of crime,
Is sympathy stuck in the cage of time?

A minute on your wrist as it freezes,
It is never meant to stop.
A rare comparison; some deep analysis,
With unlike others, gives you a drop.
Impatient hour, throws a web of fate,
Serendipity as your early prize,
Accident, if you got late.

Timid clock on its move,
Silly rhythm on which I groove,
Drives my impulse beyond control,
Extends my veins, to which they disapprove.

Silent crashes heard in a fix of time,

Sometimes identical to sheer nothingness.
An illusion in the world of mystery,
Beyond a testimony or a witness.

A circle in a minute, a minute in a circle,
Power of its hands is a profound hurdle.
Hope and despair; common and rare,
As precisely as they rhyme,
Exists in the sphere of a count,
Perpetual stretches of time .

14. Intended Us

Life was our dream colour
Changes were meant to make us suffer
Doing alright felt rather a victorious failure
Desired for night to not last forever

Blue-certainly the shade of my fantasy,
Somehow wished to escape the blue reality.
The winds of change blew in a distinct way;
While sitting near the porch, had nothing to say.

People leave themselves behind,
Hurl into a fresh new place
Risen from the rumbles of doubts in their mind
Eyes heavy, yet intended with a little left grace.

Turquoise waters and blazing sands
Gaze at the changes of the sphere-
From dull to bright in a matter of light,
Or planning away to disappear.

People go and people come-
Are we really meant to stay?
Universe is engaged; the globe evolves,
Adjust to pace and wish to ease the day.

15. An Arrow in my Rose

I am a Rose,
Rose out of the thorns.
Whilst looking for the pros,
I set my patience for the cons.

Staring at the night sky,
With my eyes all bleary,
The notion of this night thereby,
After all, is nothing- just a dreary.

A bundle of expectations that I live up for,
Shall not be an excuse for my dull sight.
This era of young wildness, as I explore,
Makes me as Obsolete as Shright.

Nurturing fragrance tends to be my fuel,
Miles to go so I keep my cool.
A savoury sparkle, when shines through my eyes,
I continue as I receive the cheers from the skies.

16. When Day becomes Night

I love the brightness, I cherish the skies–
I listen their stories and hear those lies.
Cheers to this beautiful day
Readily waiting with a coffee and smile,
Delight served in a golden tray
Perhaps, you and I are a little fragile.

Inside the blanket of strength is sick,
Amused by the elegance of applaud.
Strangely fears the sky that changes quick,
And the consequences it must have brought.

With no contradiction I shall say,
In a manner which explains my way,
I love the dark , I cherish the light.
Should accept the day, must welcome the night.

It starts with the end of it all–
Bear less worry, it is okay to fall.

After the darkest night follows a bright day,
A chance awaits irrespective of the time.
Mould your travail as smooth as clay,
Up to the expedition of triumph or paradigm.

17. If Dreams had Address

She sat on the moon, and asked the stars–
Do dreams remain beyond the sun and mars?
If they had walls, thus made of glass,
Fragile enough yet too bold to pass.

Plenty of questions, now unveil the place.
I shall seek them and find their trace.
The Nebula Street yearns for your glimpse,
Take my word and follow the hints.

The street had a park, where dreams took flight,
A spell in air, swirled to grant delight.
The shiny carousel spun in a golden hue,
Lifting her laughter where the butterflies flew.

It stretched wide beneath the sky; crimson blue
A sea of swings soared where the stardust blew
Every spin, leap and every lapse she raced,
Was a piece of her heart, she timelessly embraced.

The next halt felt like a string of fate,
Mouth left open in the awe of candy gate,
Marshmallow clouds swirled in a sugar spun sky–
Drifting like whispers as cotton floats by.

Streams of cocoa, the ranges of frozen cream,
They stunned her silence through a fever dream.
She twirled through the wonder, weightless and free,
Almost lost in a dreamland of candied ecstasy.

77th Lunar Avenue awaited the steps of her foot.
Where destiny whispered and courage took root.
A saviour of peace, light broke the chain.
For the villains who rose, shattered in vain.

From towers of moonlight, she watched her land,
A glowing might with roaring fire in hand.
At Lunar Avenue, fate found its queen–
Heroic warrior of justice, fierce and serene.

Upon a fulfilled day, she felt the warmth of home,
Soon drowned in the depths of sleep,
Yet morning waits where dreamers roam,
With endless worlds, for her to keep.

18. aEsTHetICs of being Alive

Life is small, yet big—
It deepens as much as you dig.
Like a tree, reliant on its roots,
Sweet or sour, yet colorful like its fruits.

Even a cup of tea—anyhow, it's hot to drink.
Cup of tea? Life's more gratifying than you think.
Long-lasting leisure, carefree as you recline,
Sweet, patent pleasure comes along a decline.

Stir your soul—there's more to life.
Gather more echoes; collect as archives.
Being the basic shades of a palette,
Dark and light are the one.

Like the vibe evincing through talent,
Monotonous, yet bright as the sun.
"Life's heavenly"—an old cliché,
But set your eyes on things more divine.

It is rewarding to give it a shot—
For an aesthetic life or a mulled wine.

19. Mono

Once a Girl who danced in rain
Far from distress, away from pain
Those hazel eyes, with thick lashes curled–
They shone like diamonds from some magic world.

Her innocence that could not be tamed,
Fresh and pure, like skies just rained.
When sun rose high and trees turned gold,
Her aura was native in heaven's hold.

Her heart once glittered; mind would shimmer,
Changing times turned her into a sinner.

Once a Girl who danced in rain,
Grew into a woman, shaped by pain.
Those hazel eyes, now were not so bright
Lost in shadows by some shady sight.

Purity that she once evinced through–
Wordly hardships made her blue.

Hunting butterflies treasured the young soul
Dwelling on past is now her daily role.

But still so bold, yet so mighty,
She went on for an extra mile
Of all the goals, she chose so wisely
She grabbed her nostalgic smile.

20. Where Magic meets Fate

Stars, the guides of magic,
Beams in the face of hollow.
Enchanting, yet their stories remain tragic-
Void ingestion, their fate follows.

Optimist in a sense of beauty,
Perhaps is what it seeks to become.
Guides through the midst of nights,
Through which solitary it tends to overcome.

A tale of stories which they disclose
Narratives which could compel you to ponder with force
A suite of songs, sung unusually clear
Those silent symphonies you possibly cannot hear.

The star that burns its soul
Just to paint the sky with light.
A melancholic glow gleams at the pole,
A majestic show for your leisurely night.

These graceful bodies touch their grand end;
The shallow corpse drifts and dances in cosmic sorrow.
Where magic and wonder once used to blend,
Now strives for one last night to borrow.

21. I'm Ready to Let Go

Heart warming yet loaded with gloom,
This passage could save me from the doom,
My mind directs, ahead to a path untold
The heart still lingers, too naive to be bold.

A choice that awaits, not for too long
Plain canvas, where now my destiny belongs,
In wide open sky, wings shall not rewind.
Away from longing, new freedom it shall find.

Oh! It stirs my soul, I wish to hold– no but;
Let Go! Let Go, for it aches your heart,
Let Go for another unspoiled start,
Pile your courage, for all it takes
A voice unshaken, no matter what breaks.

Let Go of the leaves that autumn sheds,
Let Go of the beauty that snow flake spreads,
Let Go of the night, the sun still awaits,
Stars were ethereal, feel the magic sunshine creates.

Let Go, its beautiful! at a cost of sorrow
Yesterday it was, while nothing for tomorrow.
Disguised as the end, is a fresh new embrace.
Through the winds of future, new hope to trace.